REVENGE OF THE CHRISTMAS BOX

A PARODY

by
Cathy Crimmins
&
Tom Maeder

DOVE
BOOKS

ISBN 0-7871-1037-X

Printed in the United States of America

Dove Books
8955 Beverly Boulevard
Los Angeles, CA 90048

Distributed by Penguin USA

Text design and layout by Carolyn Wendt
Jacket design and layout by Rick Penn-Kraus

First Printing: October 1996

10 9 8 7 6 5 4 3 2 1

TABLE OF CONTENTS

$\mathcal{I}$NTRODUCTION

he Christmas Box, a recent bestseller and instant classic, tells the simple, touching story of a young couple and their child who come to stay in the Salt Lake City mansion of an elderly widow. Through their friendship with her, and through letters discovered in a Christmas box in the attic—letters she has written to her long dead little girl—they come to realize the supreme importance of "the first gift of Christmas": the love that parents have for their children.

This bittersweet tale speaks to all of us at a very fundamental level, moving us either to tears or to nausea, which is why the book sold several million copies and seized the number one spot on both the hardcover and paperback bestseller lists.

But, like children's fairy tales, familiar to modern audiences only through Disney animated films or from nineteenth century drawing room retellings—pale, sanitized versions of the folk originals—the story of the Christmas Box has a long, varied, unexpectedly complex heritage. This simple tale exists in many different forms, some charming, some brutal, all fascinating, of which the familiar published version is but one variant.

We have devoted nearly twelve years to a contemporary folklore study of the Christmas Box story. We have traveled the country, asking people everywhere—farmers toiling in the fields, drunks in bars, television producers, office workers—to "Tell us the story of the Christmas Box." We have listened in humble awe to the extraordinarily rich array of tales our nation's fertile imagination has crafted. This is truly the voice of America.

The complete anthology of Christmas Box stories, annotated, with scholarly discussions, will be published in six volumes shortly after the Millennial Christmas Box Symposium, scheduled to be held in Salt Lake City in early 2001. But because the story of the Christmas Box is being told more and more and more and more and more, and because the people seem to have an insatiable appetite for the tale, it seemed good to publish some portion of the stories immediately.

Here, then, they are.

CATHY CRIMMINS
TOM MAEDER

THE CHRISTMAS JAR

t may be that I am getting old and senile and confused. It may be that I am getting weary of a skeptical age that pokes holes in my corny story much the same as an evil middle school student pokes out a teacher's eyes. Or, it may just be that I smell bad and nobody wants to come near me. Whatever the reason, I find that with each passing Christmas the story of the Christmas Jar is told less and needed more.

I was born in a pickle factory in the shadow of snowy mountains. Believe me, my family knew jars. Perhaps a brief dissertation on jars would be appropriate here. There are big jars and small jars. There are mayonnaise jars and peanut butter jars. The very word *jar* seems disturbing, and yet it is not: Some of our happiest moments in life are spent in front of jars. When we are little, we smile at baby food jars. As youngsters at picnics, we respond to mustard and relish jars. When we are in love, a jar of vaseline can sometimes come in handy. When we are old and dry and wrinkled, we turn to jars of moisturizer to ease our suffering. And what is a cremation urn if not a jar? Yes, we begin and end our lives surrounded by jars. And that brings me to the story of the most special jar in my life, the Christmas Jar.

We were broke and eating jars of pickled pigs' feet when Kyrie saw the ad:

Wanted: Young couple with goldfish to share home with elderly lady. Free room and board in exchange for listening to a rambling old broad lecture you about life.

"Look at this ad," said Kyrie. "Think of how much money we would save! And you're always rambling yourself, so I can certainly listen to some old fogy."

The next day we went to the trailer park where Myrtle lived. She asked us all sorts of questions: Did we like Oprah? Would we approve of her cigar smoking? What were our theories about bringing up goldfish? She said we could move into her trailer right then, even though we would all have to share a bed. It seemed like heaven to us: She was so nice, and she had cable TV. We ran back to our tiny apartment to break the news to Jenny, our goldfish.

All day long, while I built up my body-piercing business in town, Myrtle and Kyrie sat around the trailer eating potato chips, watching MTV, and taking care of Jenny. Jenny flourished in her new surroundings—she could tell that Myrtle truly loved goldfish. They built a relationship: Jenny came right up to the side of the bowl whenever Myrtle tapped her zircon ring on the glass. Often Myrtle would get misty-eyed as she sang sea chanteys to her little finned protégée. She encouraged me to read or sing to Jenny, too, but more often I was too busy or too preoccupied to think about my fish's needs.

One night as I lay between Myrtle and Kyrie, listening to their snoring, I heard something else: an angelic sound and the roar of the ocean. A figure looking like Charlie the Tuna appeared briefly, and before I knew it I was standing in front of the trailer's tiny broom closet, out from which a strong light shone. Inside, I found a beautiful frosted jar in the shape of a Christmas tree, with a tightly screwed-on lid. It was the most beautiful jar I had ever seen. The next day I told Kyrie about my experience, and she laughingly suggested that an angel had brought me to the broom closet. Myrtle, who was only a foot away in the trailer's kitchen, told me that the jar was a very old Christmas jar that people used to fill with foodstuffs during the holidays. "There is something special inside it," she said, her eyes misting up, "and if you figure out what it is, you will know the true gift of Christmas."

The next day Myrtle was run over by a group of bikers out in front of the trailer park. Kyrie called me from the hospital, but I was too busy to come right away since I had two belly buttons and five nose rings scheduled for that afternoon. One of the bikers who had run over Myrtle came into my shop to ask about a lip piercing, and he asked, "Hey, don't you live with that crazy old broad who had the dead goldfish?"

I was stunned. That night, before I visited Myrtle at the hospital, I stopped by the trailer park to look inside the Christmas jar. Nestled at the bottom, underneath some Easter grass, were two little statues of the sort you would see in a fishbowl, one of a mermaid and the other a castle. I found a yellowing paper next to them with a poem on it:

Swimmy, little Swimmy—you've gone to sea for good.
Thank you, little Swimmy, for giving me motherhood.

On a hunch, I walked from the park through the woods to the local pet cemetery. There I found, decorated with a Christmas wreath, an enormous marble monument with a giant fishbowl on top of it. The words SWIMMY—BELOVED PET OF MYRTLE, 1947–1948 were carved into its pedestal. Now I understood. Myrtle had probably known she was going to die pretty soon, and she wanted her trailer to be filled once again with the love of a young family. No wonder she had so enjoyed having our goldfish around.

I rushed to the hospital, where Myrtle was fading fast. "Myrtle," I said, "I looked inside the Christmas jar."

"Ah," she replied, gasping for breath. "So do you know what the gift of Christmas is?"

"To truly love your fish?"

"Well, something like that," she said, her eyes flipping up into her head. "Swimmy waits!" she shouted, slipping away to meet her favorite guy with gills.

After Myrtle's death, I began to truly cherish Jenny our goldfish. Of course, she died only a few months later since fish don't last that long, but I didn't even flush her down the toilet when she went. I buried her near Swimmy, and Myrtle is buried there, too, and if you come to my body piercing salon in town I can give you directions to the cemetery, where you can leave flowers or buy a goldfish from the roadside stand Kyrie now runs at Myrtle's and Swimmy's graveside.

THE CHRISTMAS BOXING HELENA

I. The Surgeon's Mansion

Some years ago I was struggling to make a living as a neophyte free-lance embalmer, but found it hard to support myself and a family on my paltry income. The perks of the profession didn't help much. My wife, Scari, felt uneasy in our coffin bed, and could never get used to the slits in the back of our shoes and clothes, specially made for dressing corpses.

"Look at this," Scari said one morning over breakfast, pointing to the classified section of the newspaper.

Deranged, reclusive, semiretired cardiovascular surgeon seeks discreet live-in couple to assist with light chores around sprawling mansion. Voluptuous yet aloof daughters always welcome. Call 555-5555. Dr. Nick Cavanaugh.

"Should we?" I said.

"If we save money on rent, perhaps we can spend it on other things, like food," Scari said.

So we went for an interview. Dr. Cavanaugh certainly was strange. Dirty, disheveled, with a wild, almost incoherent manner.

"Why did you retire at such an early age?" I dared ask. He was only about forty years old.

"Love," he said cryptically. "One does many things for love."

He questioned me closely. "Do you have friends in the police department? Do you mind sharp objects? Have an irrational aversion to amputees?"

To all, I replied in the negative.

"Then you're in," he said.

"Thank you, Dr. Cavanaugh."

"Call me Nick," he said. "I think we'll get along just fine. You know, Richard, you're a fortunate man. You have a beautiful wife who loves you."

"Thank you, Nick."

"Lovely woman. Tall woman. Nice legs."

I can't say why, but his compliments made me vaguely uneasy.

II. The Hidden Box

We moved in. It wasn't hard.

"Hey, Nick," I said, "I see our wing of the mansion is already furnished. You mind if we store some of our possessions in the attic?"

He didn't. He was the soul of hospitality. "My attic is your attic," he said.

Of course, we didn't have any possessions. We had already pawned everything we owned. And we had also pawned lots of things we didn't own. I was always on the lookout for supplementary income. Face it— rich people are scum! By taking advantage of them, we turn their otherwise worthless lives into something moderately useful, like a natural resource. So I was prospecting, so to speak—mining the doctor's attic for what it was worth.

Those old clothes would bring a little at the thrift shop. Somebody's jewelry chest—make a note to have that appraised. Child's train set in good condition, with original package—check with Bill about that toy auction down in Pennsylvania next month.

And then, very faintly, off in one corner, I heard someone singing "Hello, m' baby." Could it be true, I wondered? The frog in the cornerstone from the old cartoon? That would bring a fortune. I shifted twenty years of *National Geographic*s, outdated high school and medical texts, the flotsam and jetsam of a life gone by. Finally I came to a large box covered by a satin sheet, which seemed to be the source of the singing. I was about to lift the sheet when I heard Nick clomping up the stairs. He was carrying a tray of food and looked surprised to see me.

"Oh, Richard, I didn't know you were up here."

I stared at the tray in puzzlement.

"Oh, this? I like to eat in the attic sometimes. I'm crazy as a loon, you know. It's just one of my little idiosyncrasies."

I went back downstairs. Scari was out. It seemed she was always out these days, gadding about. When I protested she said, "Oh, Richard, I get lonely sometimes. You get to work with people all day. I don't."

I pointed out that the people I worked with were dead.

"Well, of course they are, Richard. You can't embalm living people, you silly." She laughed at me. Our marriage was suffering. I was neglecting my wife for my work, but you can't start a new business without putting in the time.

III. Dinner

A few days after our arrival, Nick invited us to join him for dinner. It was, like everything else in the place, a curious affair. The meal itself consisted of nothing but some type of meat. The utensils were all medical instruments—scalpels, clamps, forceps, and many others that I could not even identify. Nick wielded them deftly, cleanly dissecting his food and transplanting it to his mouth, while Scari and I labored more slowly, clumsily, with an element of fear.

"Your work and mine are rather similar, Richard," Nick said conversationally. "Except that you bury your successes as well as your mistakes." He observed me hacking away at my meat with the scalpel. "Your technique shows promise, but no discipline. I could give you a few pointers sometime, if you like."

"You said you retired from medicine for love, Nick," I said, the wine making me bold. "Would it be rude of me to ask you to tell us about it? Nowadays one rarely hears of people being motivated by the nobler emotions."

"It was a great love, Richard. Helena was her name. You remind me of her a bit, Scari," Nick said. "But you are much taller."

"What happened?" Scari asked.

"She came apart," Nick said. Then, curiously, he corrected himself. "I mean to say…we drifted apart."

"That's so sad," Scari said.

Nick looked at me fixedly. He waved his scalpel in the air for emphasis. "Richard, remember one of the first rules ever given to man: A man shall 'cleave unto his wife.' From the second book of Genesis. That's a favorite quote of mine, but I've always found it strange, etymologically speaking. *Cleave* is one of those extraordinary words that means opposite things—to cut apart and to stick together. Do we stay together by chopping apart? I wonder. I wonder. ..."

After dinner I returned to the funeral home for a while. I had a stiff to stuff. Scari said she needed some air and went for a walk.

IV. A Dreamy Venus de Milo

That night I dreamed that Scari came home at 3:00 A.M. reeking of cheap whisky, with her blouse buttoned wrong and her makeup smeared all over her face. I had similar dreams every night for a week. They were so vivid I could have sworn they were real, but Scari assured me I was fast asleep, thrashing and moaning, and that she spent long hours speaking soothing words and stroking my feverish brow. She is an angel.

The pressures of work kept me from returning to the attic. My business was growing in a most gratifying way. It was the Christmas season, and drunk drivers smashed into each other and mowed down innocent pedestrians, supplying me with a never-ending stream of corpses in need of restoration and preservation. But my friend Bill kept bugging me about getting stuff to him for the auction, so I went back. Once again, after a few minutes, I heard the faint strains of singing. This time it was "The Hokey Pokey." I listened carefully to make sure that Nick was not coming, and then rummaged around until I found the mysterious box. I lifted off the sheet.

The box had a bottom, back, and two sides, but no top or front, and was lined with plush velvet. In it was a beautiful woman, a real Venus de Milo, with no arms or legs.

"Hey, big boy," she said when she saw me, and laughed.

"Oh, my God!" I said, stepping back in horror.

"Yeah, I know, it takes a little getting used to. Imagine how it was for me."

She sang a little more of her song. "It's *our* song. Nick's and mine. He would hold me close and we danced through the night."

I found it touching to imagine an armless, legless woman doing the Hokey Pokey.

In the quiet attic, Helena—for it was she—told me her story: how Nick once dated her, adored her; she dumped him, he stalked her, he finally lured her to his house; there was a speeding car; then she woke to find he had amputated her legs, later whittled off a bit more to keep her in line.

"So what are you doing up here?"

"Of course, I hated him at first, but then…you know…the Stockholm syndrome and all…I fell in love with my captor. My momma always told me to play hard to get, but that's not easy to do in my condition. And as soon as he knew he had me, he lost interest. He stuck me up here a few years ago and now he just visits at mealtimes. He only takes me out at Halloween, to scare the kids in the neighborhood."

"What do you do with your time, Helena?"

"I tried knitting, but that was a foolish dream. You can imagine how frustrating it was. I used to read, but it gets kind of boring when you have to wait five hours for someone to turn the page. I watch a lot of television, and when Nick's in a bad mood he leaves it on PBS all the time. He says one day he may buy me one of those telephone headsets and I can get a job doing telemarketing. I think that would be lots of fun. It would be exciting to have a career."

"This is terrible, Helena," I said.

"It happens," she replied.

Later that day I told Scari about my discovery.

"I think you should mind your own business, Richard. This is between the two of them. It's not our place to interfere."

She was right, of course, but I felt so sorry for Nick and Helena.

V. *Anatomy 101*

The dreams grew worse. I dreamed that Scari didn't come home for days on end, and that I once saw her walking down the street arm in arm with two sailors.

"Don't be ridiculous," Scari said when I mentioned my dreams to her. "Oh, by the way, do you have a hundred dollars? I need to go to the grocery store."

I dreamed that she was always asking for grocery money, but that she never bought any groceries, and that her shopping trips always lasted overnight, when the store was closed.

Nick spent long hours sitting in the parlor, either studying Genesis 2:24 or honing some sharp instrument, his only other pastime.

"Nick…Scari and I seem to be drifting apart. I'm worried."

"Remember that command, Richard. Cleave unto her."

"I'm not sure I understand, Nick. I don't have a clue how to solve our problems."

"Solomon had a way of solving problems. It involved cleaving, too. Say, Richard, would you like that dissecting lesson we talked about?"

"Sure!" I said. We went down to his basement workshop, where he taught me to make quick, deft incisions, to clamp and ligate, to tease apart tissue planes, to suture flawlessly.

"This is a wonderful skill, Richard. Not only will it help you in your work, but it's a hobby that you can share with the one you love."

"By the way, Nick, I met Helena," I said.

"She's a lovely girl, isn't she, Richard?"

"Lovely. Yes."

"Helena and I have had our good times and bad, Richard. I've neglected her. But I'm going to make it up. I'm giving her a custom-made Vuitton carrying case for Christmas. And then I'm going to take her on a trip around the world."

"I know she'll like that, Nick."

VI. Cleavage

Nick's trip around the world was not to be. One cold, snowy day in January, the men in the white coats came and took him away.

I went to visit him a week later in the nuthouse. He was an emaciated shadow of his former self.

"Take care of Helena for me," he said. "Promise."

I promised.

"And remember, Richard: *cleave.*"

"I will."

When Scari came home that afternoon—the first time I had seen her in several days—I told her of my visit to Nick.

"I think you and Helena will get along well. You'll find that you have a lot in common."

I invited her down to the basement to see something.

Epilogue

Nick's example and fine words served me well. My bad dreams stopped, and my relationship with Scari suddenly improved.

I bought a double stroller, and on sunny days Helena, Scari, and I all go for walks around the neighborhood.

Eventually Nick improved enough that the nuthouse allows him out on day passes. Sometimes we double-date.

THE CHRISTMAS
BOX OFFICE

he ad in *Variety* was intriguing:

> *Octogenarian actor with large Bel Air house seeks live-in couple*
> *for late-night talks about the industry, cigar shopping, and*
> *preparation of light poolside snacks. Private quarters, own cel-*
> *lular phone, and Humvee provided. Photogenic, wisecracking*
> *child welcome.*

"It's us!" said my wife Kelli, looking up from the bookstand on her exercise bike.

"What is?"

"This ad."

I hit the pause button on the *Buns of Steel* video I was watching and grabbed the paper from her. She was right—the ad sure looked good. We had always wanted to move up in zip codes, but the last few years had been rough. I had made a big splash as a producer of a talking pig movie in my late twenties, but then *Mother Jones* did an exposé a few months later with graphic photos of the dozens of dead piglets that had been electronically stimulated to feign animation on the set. "You'll Never Eat Pork in This Town Again," the piece was called, and it ruined me. I couldn't even produce infomercials: The best I got was an occasional chance to do videos of liposuctions and tummy tucks for plastic surgeons who would then trade a free procedure for Kelli or me. At least we looked good (the best we had ever looked!), but financially we were going down.

The only bright spot in all of it had been our five-year-old daughter Cauliflower. She was one of those perky *Full House*–type tykes with a precocious vocabulary and a simpering smile that endeared her to the camera. We had started her acting early—she was the fetus in the ultrasound they showed in that drippy Michael Keaton movie about the dying daddy—and her career had been steadily blossoming when my dead-pig scandal hit. So we did what any Hollywood parents would do. We changed her name. Not her first name: We were too inordinately proud of being the first people on our block to name our kid after a vegetable. (Did you see that "Cauliflower" was on Madonna's short list of girls' baby names?) Instead, we changed Cauliflower's last name—to Phoenix. Few people keep track of how many Phoenix kids there actually are, and how wacky their names got as the mom kept whelping. Cauliflower Phoenix gets a lot of calls.

Still, Cauli, as we call her, couldn't earn enough to support us in our customary style. Kelli and Cauli were always after me to go to Aspen, to buy a house in Litchfield, to buy a llama ranch, and I just couldn't do it on the ever-decreasing residuals from my pork project and from Cauli's fees as a child model and Nickelodeon game show star. Maybe, I thought, Kelli was right—we could use a move, and especially one that had career possibilities.

"You know I'm great at preparing poolside snacks," said Kelli, "and Cauli could entertain the old man with all her songs and animal riddles. Maybe you could finally get back to your real love, writing, and do a screenplay about the friendship between an octogenarian actor and an adorable little girl."

So we made an appointment to meet George Burnside, the diminutive ex-vaudevillian, in his beautiful Bel Air mansion. I was shocked at how diminutive he really was—the cigar he was smoking was nearly half his height. But I was charmed immediately by his warmth and pluckiness. Kelli and Cauli, too, fell in love with him instantly.

"Hear the one about the man who walked through the screen door and strained himself?" he said to our little daughter, and she burst into gales of childish laughter.

"I know a woman who sleeps with cats—Mrs. Katz!!!" he screamed to Kelli, who nearly fell over giggling.

I have to say I never really found him funny, sort of more in the pathetic vein. Yet we decided to move in, even though I had my doubts initially. My two girls were happy, I had a great zip code, and we had oodles of room and our own Humvee to tool around town in. I guess you could say it was one of the best times of my life, except that George hounded me constantly.

"You don't know the true meaning of Christmas, do ya, kid?" he would say, chomping at his two-foot cigar.

"You're Jewish, aren't you, George? What the hell are you talking about? You're *meshuga*!" I would say, knowing I could distract him with any Yiddish and get him to launch into one of his dozens of bad Jewish jokes. But eventually he would return to the subject.

"The true meaning, the *true* meaning of Christmas," George would whine. "Someday you're gonna find out, believe me, and then you'll be sitting pretty."

George had an attic full of all his old vaudeville props and movie costumes. Cauli and I liked to go up there to play sometimes. There were old seltzer bottles and clown shoes and boxes of cigar stubs that had been smoked by famous people like Jack Benny and Fanny Brice. He had all his old love letters to his wife, Grady, stowed away in a beautiful old trunk, and sometimes I would swipe them from the trunk and read them to Kelli late at night. They were pretty hot stuff, and I would make believe that I had written them—Kelli would be like putty in my hands after that. So the old coot, disgusting as he was with his cigars and his leers and his off-color, pathetically unfunny jokes, really helped my sex life. I've got to hand him that.

Tragically, our idyll was soon to end. George, it seems, had fallen ill with something called Vaudeville Hunch, a terminal condition in which he shticked himself to death in delirious fits of joke after joke. Each joke took at least a quarter inch off his spinal column, and when they finally took him away in the ambulance, he was only a foot and a half tall and each of his internal organs was the size of a pea. As they were strapping him onto the gurney, George looked me in the eye and gasped, "Kid, kid...you still don't know, do ya?"

"Know what?" I said.

"The true meaning of your Christmas."

"No," I said slowly. "I'm sorry...I guess I don't, George."

"Look at the bottom of the trunk, kid. I'll be seeing you. Don't take any wooden nickels."

Kelli, Cauli, and I stood and watched as the glowing red lights of the ambulance receded in the distance. Cauli was inconsolable. "He was the funniest man I ever knew, Papa," she cried as we watched old Three Stooges movies late into the night.

That night, after Cauli and Kelli finally fell asleep, I tried to drift off myself, but I kept hearing sounds coming from the attic. When I climbed the stairs, I could discern old Al Jolson songs coming from the vicinity of the trunk full of George's love letters. As I lifted the lid, a false bottom popped up to reveal a neat stack of scripts—at least a dozen of them. On the title page of each, where the screenwriter's name should have been, were the words "YOUR NAME HERE." I whistled softly. So this was what the old man was talking about!

Kelli, Cauli, and I went to visit George several times that last week of his life. He just kept getting tinier. On the night before he died, he was so little I could hold him in the palm of my hand. He smiled and attempted to do a little soft-shoe across the base of my thumb. "That's me," he cracked, "George Burnside...smaller than life!"

Then he got more serious. "Ya found 'em, right, kid?"

"Yes, George, I did, but I don't understand."

"Those scripts are gold, kid! Box office gold. I had enough money already...what was I gonna do with 'em? I wanted to find a young ambitious schmuck like you, someone with a family that could really enjoy all the trappings of success. I thought I would give them to you. It's my Christmas gift. Just remember to release the movies at the right time. There's nothing like the Christmas box office receipts!"

We buried little George in a cigar box, and I went on to be the successful producer of a dozen films with receipts each over $230 million. It was all there in his trunk—scripts that turned out to be a gold mine. Spielberg had nothing on me. Schwarzenegger and Jim Carrey and Brad Pitt were begging to be in my pictures.

$

In the end, everything went just fine. Kelli and I got divorced, but she's married to an Arabian potentate now and happy as a lark. I had a bad time there for a while after my sex change operation, but Michael Jackson and I have been living together for three years now, and I think it will last. Cauli acted in three of my films, was on the cover of every magazine in America, and went into rehab a couple of times. Now she is an animal rights activist and the chairwoman of the George Burnside Cigars for the Third World Committee. She says she'll never forget her hilarious Uncle George and just did the voice-over for the short documentary: "Waiter, There's a Fly in My Soup: The Gustatory Humor of George Burnside."

And me—I, too, think of George all the time. He taught me that nothing is more important than money and success. He taught me what the Christmas Box Office is all about.

THE CHRISTMAS ICEBOX

[A fragment.]

…Over in the corner of the attic I perceived a small, elongated, metallic cylinder, with a glass plate inset at one end and a dizzying assortment of pipes and dials at the other.

"She's such a sweet old lady," my wife, Ditzi, called from the far side of the attic. "I bet we find something really neat and touching, like a box full of letters she wrote to her dead baby long ago."

I moved closer to the cylinder. It reminded me of something I had seen in science fiction movies.

"Oh, won't it be profoundly moving, honey? Maybe you could even write a book about it," Ditzi said.

The glass pane was covered with frost. I reached out and rubbed it away with the sleeve of my jacket.

"Maybe the book would be a bestseller, and then you could ditch that silly old business of yours. We could even afford to send the kid to boarding school and go on a cruise around the world," Ditzi said. She was such a romantic.

"Oh, my God!" I said.

"What do you say, honey?" Ditzi asked.

"Ditzi, it's not letters to her baby," I cried. "That old lady has cryogenically frozen the baby itself. Her little angel is right here, waiting to be thawed out when a cure is discovered!"

THE CHRISTMAS CAT LITTER BOX

always wished I was allergic to cats. I can't stand them, but my wife, Feli, loves the little hair balls. We had only been married a year and we already had four of the furry moochers hanging around the house costing me way too much money. Every week, Feli would come home with hundreds of dollars of cat paraphernalia, until finally I laid down the law: Either the cats had to go, or me. We simply couldn't afford to harbor the beasts.

The next day Feli saw an ad in our local paper:

Slightly lunatic old cat lady seeks young couple to feed and care for her and her 160 felines. Entire mansion at your disposal and twenty-four-hour access to fresh catnip. Kitties welcome!

"This is wonderful!" she said. "We could live rent-free and have a great environment for our little furry family."

Feli dragged me off immediately to meet the old biddy. Her house reeked of cat urine even from the driveway. Wretched pussies roamed around every room, sat on every couch and atop every table. Feli smiled throughout it all as I started feeling mildly sick to my stomach.

"Meow," said the old lady, Caterina, smiling at us in a loopy way. "That's like *aloha* in kitten talk. Come here, you big old beauty," she said, resting an old black Persian tomcat up on her lap. "Mommy's itty-bitty baby doll kit-kit!"

I excused myself, ostensibly to go to the bathroom, but really more to get out of her claustrophobic living room. I began exploring the house and found cats in every room, even the closets. Finally, on the third floor, I saw a tiny, rickety staircase leading up to a ceiling trap-door. Something compelled me to climb it and enter Caterina's attic.

I took a deep breath and knew that something was different. No cats! No cat hair! No smell of cat piss! The attic was filled with beautiful furniture, none of it damaged by the deadly claws of felines. And yet, there was some evidence that cats had once been there. In the center of this tranquil setting was a beautiful brass inlaid box filled with sand and what I can only describe as mummified cat turds, hard as rocks and odorless. Strewn through the sand were small strands of what looked like Christmas tinsel.

I sat for a while in the quiet attic, meditating on my marriage. Feli, I felt, loved her cats far more than she loved me. I had made a mistake in marrying her, but it wasn't too late to get out of it. I would leave Feli and go in search of a woman with no pets or, at least, only one dog. Feli was young and would find another husband. I got up and began to move toward the stairs and then decided to perform one kind gesture for the dotty lady downstairs. I picked up the brass kitty litter box—man, was it heavy!—and carted it downstairs to the kitchen, where I emptied its contents and washed it out with Lysol.

Feli and the old woman, Caterina, came in to the kitchen to fetch some tea.

"I thought I'd help you out a bit," I said, pointing to the clean, gleaming brass box.

"Oh, my God!" screamed Caterina. "My Snowball's last litter box! Now I have nothing left in the world!" She fell to the ground and sank into a coma, never to recover.

It seems that everyone in the town except me knew the sad story of Caterina's devotion to Snowball. Ten years ago he had been her only cat, her pride and joy. Then he had been run over by a UPS truck on Christmas Eve. She had buried him in the pet cemetery under a statue of a giant catnip mouse, his favorite toy. (You can still see the statue in the pet cemetery right off the Jersey Turnpike in Newark, where it has come to represent all beloved pets lost in highway accidents.) Yet Caterina kept Snowball's last litter box, which he had decorated with the many strands of tinsel he had eaten the week before Christmas. She actually lived in the attic, where she did not allow the hundreds of cats she sheltered to roam. Even though she would adopt any stray and give it a home, it would never take the place in her heart that Snowball occupied.

Shortly after I performed my misguided good deed, Caterina died. She had no family, so Feli and I had her cremated and scattered her ashes among the twenty-five litter boxes in the mansion. Feli moved into the house and became the official new crazy cat lady of our town, and I took off across the country in search of a new life. I still tell the story of the Christmas Litter Box to anyone who will listen, even though I don't have the faintest idea of what it means.

The Christmas Vox

A YULETIDE EXPLORATION OF PHONE SEX

by St. Nicholas Baker

The Phone Call Begins

"What are you wearing?" he asked.

She said, "Red and white. I'm wearing a white frilly blouse, a red dirndl skirt, white wool tights with jingle bells sewn into them, and reindeer-leather boots I got for just nine dollars."

"What are you doing?"

"I'm lying on my bed."

"What kind of bed?"

"A sleigh bed…antique. It's made. I'm lying on top of a fur throw. A few months ago some of the little guys gave me a fur throw, and it's been folded up in the closet ever since. I was feeling guilty, so I took it out and put it on top of the bed."

"The little guys? Do you live in a commune?"

"Sort of. But nothing kinky, if that's what you mean."

"Oh. I'm relieved. Somehow a fur throw seems like…well, I don't know…a sort of intimate gift, you know? I think of fur and I think of those sexy catalogs…."

"You mean like *Furry Personal*?"

"Yeah, that catalog. I get it once in a while, but I really can't imagine giving a woman fur underwear."

"It could get kind of messy. Well, it *does* get kind of messy. Actually, I know, because where I come from it's a tradition to wear fur undies on your wedding night."

"So you were married?"

"Ummm?"

"Are you still?"

"Does it matter?"

"I guess not. Where are you from?"

"An arctic city."

"Really. Well, I'm from a Southern city. What are you doing alone on Christmas Eve?"

"Oh, I'm always alone on Christmas Eve."

The Anatomical Terms

"*Fruitcakes.* I like to call them *fruitcakes,*" he said.

"I see. And are there any other terms you use, to yourself, for the breasts?"

"Oh… sugarplums, gumdrops, packages, ORNAMENTS."

"Why all the Christmas terms?"

"I don't know. I think Christmas was my happiest time as a child, so I link sexual joy with those terms. Let's not get overly analytical, please. So how big are your fruitcakes?"

"Very big. We grow 'em big up here."

"Nice. So how about you? Any special words for the male organ?"

"Gee, no one has ever asked me that before. But, now that you mention it…yes."

"So?"

"Well, maybe this is karma or something: My nicknames are a lot like yours. When I'm diddling myself, I think of a man's…um…*yule log*. Or his *candy cane*."

"Sounds like we were made for each other."

The Climax

"So I've got my candy cane up between your big luscious fruitcakes, and we're caroling, caroling, caroling…"

"Joy to the world…I'm about to come.…"

"Round yon virgin…"

"Ooooooh!"

[The sound of jingle bells and a deep, hearty male voice: "Ho ho ho! I'm home, honey!"]

"Damn! The old man's here!"

"Old man?"

"How could we possibly talk this long? Gotta go. Call into this

phone service next Christmas Eve. It's the only time I can ever be sure
we're alone. Keep your yule log lit for me!"

　　[Sound of a phone hanging up.]

The Christmas Polyhedron

hristmas around our house was always a nightmare. My wife, Proofi, was a mathematician, and always had some geometrical objection to everything.

"A Christmas *box,* you say? Are you sure it was a *box*? What do you mean by a *box*? Do you mean that it was a cube? Or perhaps merely a rectangular solid? Or possibly a parallelepiped? A fool like you wouldn't know the difference. For all I know, it could be a Christmas tetrahedron, or a hexahedron, or an octahedron, or a dodecahedron. No, I'll bet it's an icosahedron. The Christmas Icosahedron!"

"I don't know," I said, eager to get on with the story of my discovery in the attic. "It was just a box."

"Nothing can be just a box," Proofi replied. "What are its properties? I don't mean how *big* is it—size, Richard, does not matter—but how is it defined mathematically, in absolute terms? If you were communicating with someone from another galaxy by radio, and had no common experiences except the most fundamental logical rules and physical principles, how would you describe this—as you call it—this *Christmas Box*?"

At that point I killed her. Or rather, to satisfy her fussy sense of things, I introduced a sharp object perpendicularly through the plane that was tangent to her chest. Her vertical orientation gradually declined toward the horizontal until she was—logically, mathematically, geometrically, trigonometrically, topologically, algebraically, statistically, and in every other way—dead.

I was acquitted of the murder charge, of course: found not guilty by reason of tedium. Years later I remarried. She was another mathematician, as it happened. On our wedding night she overcame her timidity and asked about my first marriage. So I began to tell her the story of the Christmas Box.

"A Christmas *box*, you say?" she said. "Are you sure it was a *box*? What do you mean by a *box*? Do you mean that it was a cube? Or perhaps merely a rectangular solid? Or possibly a parallelepiped...."

THE CHRISTMAS
BLACK BOX

s an investigator for the Federal Aviation Agency, I've done a lot of work over the holidays, naturally. More people are flying hither and yon, and that means more wreckage for me to plough through, and more black boxes for me to pry open. Yet the minute I got the call on Christmas day, I knew this one was special.

As I hung up the phone, my wife Cessna was still gathering up the last of the wrapping paper under the tree. I came up behind her, encircling her waist for a quick hug. It wasn't easy, since she was eight and a half months pregnant.

"You've got to leave, huh?" she said sadly.

"Hell of a time to go down, don't you think? From what they're telling me, this was a tiny aircraft, too. I don't know what he was doing out in a raging snowstorm on Christmas Eve. I bet they'll find out he was one of those ultralight aircraft fanatics."

"Then go," said Cessna. "Only I hope it won't happen again. By this time next year, Santa Claus should be dropping by with bundles of presents for our baby!"

I flew to Bozeman, Montana, where Hank Regent, our Western coordinator, picked me up in his jeep. "Glad you could make it, Jim.

There's not much left there, but he wasn't a complete crackpot. He had a radio. He was trying to contact the ranger's station over at Yellowstone. So maybe we'll find some clues."

We drove to the site, where the state troopers were sifting through the wreckage. One of them, a tall blond fellow with a crew cut, approached me with a puzzled look on his face.

"Inspector," he said, extending his hand. "Officer Noel Singer. Hell of a way to spend a holiday, eh? We've been waiting for you to decipher some of this stuff."

Hank and I began walking along with him, picking our way through wood shards and masses of bloody tufts of fuzz. "Why all the fur?" I asked.

"The nearest we can tell, sir, is that the plane came down in the middle of a herd of deer or moose."

"But the bits of leather?"

"That we don't know. Even found a few bells…maybe they were pet deer, or llamas that had wandered out from somebody's ranch."

"What about the body?" I asked.

A funny look crossed Officer Noel Singer's chiseled features. "Well, that's odd, too. We know someone was flying the thing, but there's hardly any blood and guts around. Some stiff white body hair, and the innards seem to have turned all mushy. We tried to collect it, and about all we got was a bowlful of jelly."

"Hey, Noel, come take a look at this," said one of the searchers who was wearing a ski mask and a big orange ski suit.

Hank, Noel, and I went scurrying over to a spot with overturned metal runners. The orange-suited guy was extracting a small black box, about eight inches square, from the rubble.

"Well, I'll be damned," said Hank. "You hardly ever see a black box on anything less than a jet. This guy was some aviation nut, that's for sure. But this is probably a toy. I doubt that it was really recording anything."

Perhaps a brief dissertation on black boxes is in order here. I have personally examined dozens of them. The black box: symbol of disaster, the dark mysterious remnant of a pilot's last moments. I have been a pilot, and I know how much of a pilot's life is spent hurtling toward the Black Box. But isn't it just that way with everyone? We came out of a black box, and we shall return to one. We record our moments on this earth with little black boxes—what are the photos and tapes, the beeper messages, if not a foreshadowing of the Ultimate Black Box to which we will all sink some day?

I keep black boxes everywhere—in the glove compartment of my car, in the refrigerator, on my night table, in the shower. Like everyone else, I don't know when my final moments will occur. But I want them to be recorded for posterity, especially now that I will have a child. If I'm going to choke on a ham sandwich or slip on a bar of soap, I want my future son or daughter to know exactly what I was thinking as I passed beyond the portals of this mortal veil. And, just in case Cessna dies in childbirth, I make her wear a black box around her neck at all times, too. A good black box is a legacy to those who come after, a way to help the next generation learn from your mistakes.

But back to the black box at hand. This one was unlike any other black box I had ever seen. The top was ornately decorated with etchings depicting snow-covered mountains, waterfalls, and cozy cottages with smoke wafting out of rustic chimneys. Using my pen knife, I jimmied open the lock to see if there was any real electronic equipment inside. As soon as the lock broke, the lid sprang open and two candy canes and a marshmallow snowman popped out. Underneath, sitting on top of green tissue paper, was a Fisher-Price "My First Tiny Recorder," its little red "record" button still blinking.

Hank whistled. "Well, I'll be damned. It's gotta be a hoax."

I wanted to agree, but a cold chill shot up my spine as soon as I hit the rewind button. About thirty seconds later I heard an eerily familiar, jolly voice:

"Ho ho ho! Whoa! A little bit of turbulence there. Steady, boys. Now what are you doing there, Prancer? You leave Comet alone. No! Stop biting his foot. Comet! Prancer! You'll get the reins all bollixed up. AAAAAH! Now see what you've done? Goin' down. Stupid reindeer! Bad, bad. No hay for you tonight. You're the death of me, boys! What a world, what a world. Please, Mrs. Santa...be happy...I forgive you for that fling you had with the Jolly Green Giant."

I couldn't bear listening to the static at the end of the tape. Every black box has the same unhappy ending, even those carried by jolly old elves.

I returned home to Cessna a sadder but wiser man. As we lay together on our living room sofa, I fondled the black box around her neck and told her the sad story of Santa's last flight.

"And to think that I never believed in him, anyway," said Cessna.

"Never believed?" I said incredulously. I realized, at that moment, the gift that Santa had given the world: a black box proving his existence. How ironic that only his death would confirm his magical life! The Christmas Black Box would challenge everyone to carry on Santa's great work on his or her own.

The next day I sold the story about Mrs. Santa and the Jolly Green Giant to the *National Enquirer* for $350,000—I only did it for our future baby's college tuition. I know Santa would have wanted it that way.

THE CHRISTMAS SOAPBOX

Being a fragment of a play containing the impassioned oration of a renegade Elf in Santa's Workshop[*]

Fellow elves:

I stand before you, like yourselves, a victim of oppression, a slave of the arctic sweatshops perpetuated by the imperialist tyrant, the so-called Saint Nicholas. A saint—huh! More like Satan himself, as anyone can see when you unscramble his evil moniker. St. Nicholas, a.k.a. Santa Claus, the notorious boss without a country, an overgrown steroid-enhanced evil elf who answers to no law.

Where was OSHA when our brothers breathed the endless fumes of epoxy while making plastic wagons? Where were the child labor laws when thousands of our little elves perished in the famous Washable Marker experiments, where they were chained to walls for days and forced to scribble endlessly?

And there are far sadder stories. Who does not know of our dear elf friend Game Boy, whose mind was drained while he slept to create

---

[*] *This fragment was discovered in a ruined shed somewhere south of the Arctic Circle. Post-Santa scholars speculate that the jolly old elf's crash might have been connected in some way to the political unrest that seemed to be taking place at the North Pole at the time. (See "The Christmas Black Box," page 41.)*

the data for a handheld arcade toy? Or the terrible fate of the Jenny Gymnasts, our tiny elf daughters who held their legs up in the air for hours just so Santa's evil marketing team could create a prototype product for a battery-operated tumbling dolly? I know you remember, as I do, all our junior elves who died during the Silly Putty edibility experiments.

Elves, unite!!! I stand upon this Christmas Soapbox calling for an end to our distress, and a return to the true meaning of Christmas, a Christmas without the Bearded Tyrant, the Red Menace, the Roly-Poly Rat who puts in his face-time once a year, honing his popularity from the sufferings of our people.

The Christmas Pox

I. The Doctor's Mansion

Not too many years ago, my wife, Nursi, and I moved to Salt Lake City to set up a little family medical center. Malpractice suits and HMOs had driven medicine into the ground, and so we were struggling hard to make ends meet and to pay for our matching Jaguars, club member-ships, fancy clothes, rare wine collection, and two vacation homes. We knew that we had to economize, but where? We were right down to the bone as it was and couldn't sacrifice any more without compromising our investments or putting a crimp in our lifestyle.

One day Nursi was browsing through the county medical society journal when she ran across a classified ad:

> *Elderly physician seeks young medical couple for light house-keeping and occasional research duties. Call Dr. Maury Parken.*

We talked it over for a few moments, but there was really no debate. We would be able to sell our condo and put the proceeds into some business that would serve the underprivileged community, like a pawn-shop or check-cashing service. We called Dr. Parken and made an appointment to see him.

Dr. Parken was a charming old gent with flowing silvery hair, an aging-yet-still-elegant London-tailored suit, a gold watch on a long chain draped across his expansive vest, and Italian-made shoes. He was a doctor as doctors should be.

"You young folks don't know how it was," Dr. Parken told us as we sat in the parlor for our interview. "Back in my day there was no insurance, no informed consent, no consumerism. We doctors did whatever we wanted, charged what we liked, and no matter what the outcome of the case the families all snuffled and groveled around saying how grateful they were for everything we had done, which usually was just to let nature takes its course. *That* was the Golden Age of Medicine."

Nursi and I smiled sadly, sympathetically. We had heard it all before. We knew that we had strayed into a degraded profession run by pencil-pushers, and that we were little more than retail peddlers of packaged drugs and medical gadgetry. Before long the chiropractors, acupuncturists, and health food stores would take over what tattered shreds of medicine remained, so we had to make our millions fast and get the hell out.

"And back in my day we had *real* diseases," Dr. Parken ranted on. "Not these airy-fairy little things you call diseases nowadays. My patients hacked and wheezed and festered and rotted before my very eyes. The medicines *I* used were real, manly, heroic medicines, as likely to kill as to cure." He scratched his head thoughtfully. "Maybe *more* likely to kill. I was *proud* to call myself a doctor!"

Maury Parken was a strange, exalted, rather deluded man. But Nursi and I liked him. He would provide color in our bland, pampered lives. He offered spacious accommodations in exchange for hardly any work. What's more, we learned that he had no family at all, suggesting that if we endeared ourselves to him and behaved in a totally selfless way, he might leave us his mansion and fortune when he died.

II. The Lunatic at the Dinner Table

Every morning, old Dr. Maury Parken would sit in the front parlor weeping and sobbing over ancient medical texts, and then wander off to visit neighborhood cemeteries. Occasionally, after he departed I'd glance at the books he had been reading, lying tearstained on a velvet cushion. They were always left open to the sections on infectious disease, with engravings or murky photographs of leprosy, advanced syphilis, tubercular organs, gangrenous flesh.

Strange, I thought. What was going on? I wondered.

"Have you ever been to Saranac?" Dr. Parken asked us over dinner on our first evening in his house.

"Uh, I think we were there one summer when we were traveling around Europe," I bluffed. It sounded like some lakeside resort in Switzerland.

"No, Saranac, New York. I grew up there." Dr. Parken poured himself a large glass of cognac and lit a cigar. "It was a town built around a sanitorium. Wonderful place. Consumptives everywhere, coughing blood, wasting away, dying like flies. What a wonderful, memorable childhood." He stared blissfully into space for so long that I thought he was in a trance. "That's what made me want to go into medicine," he said at long last. "But…"

"What happened?" Nursi asked.

"Antibiotics!" Maury shouted, slamming his fist on the table, hard. The glasses jumped as I almost fell off my chair in surprise. He drained his glass in a single gulp, coughed until his face turned purple, and then dropped his head in his arms and cried. I glanced at Nursi, and cranked one finger around near my temple to indicate that I thought the guy was nuts.

"Antibiotics!" Maury shouted again, leaping to his feet and hurling his glass across the room. He paused, suddenly calm, and fixed me with a stare. "Who is the greatest villain of all time?"

I hated guessing games. I never got the right answer. "Hitler?" I said. I actually thought I might have a chance.

"Ha! A rank amateur," Maury snorted in disgust.

"Stalin?"

"Ha, ha! No, my young friend, the greatest villain of all time was Alexander Fleming, the discoverer of penicillin. Hitler and Stalin killed their millions, but Fleming has wiped out billions, trillions, quadrillions, quintillions…"

"I don't get it," Nursi said.

"Bacteria!" the doctor sobbed. "Antibiotics are killing bacteria, the poor little things. Their little corpses strewn everywhere." His eyes lit up with radiant fury. "And does anyone dig graves for them? Does anyone put marble angels on the grave of *Haemophilus influenzae*? Do poets write touching epitaphs for all the little *Streptococcus pneumoniae,* ripped from life at such a tender young age? Or cute little *Yersinia pestis*… no one to mourn the little rodlike fellows.… Do you see little *Salmonella*'s face on the side of a milk carton when it vanishes? No, of course not! Milk cartons themselves are grotesque monuments to that bactericidal maniac Pasteur and his vile ways!"

I yawned loudly and stretched ostentatiously. "Well, Dr. Parken, that was a lovely meal and this has been a fascinating conversation, but I think I'll have to turn in. I have a long day tomorrow...." Nursi took my cue and yawned and stretched and said that she did, too.

"You think I'm crazy, don't you?"

"Oh, no, no, Dr. Parken," I said, humoring him. "Of course we don't think you're crazy."

"Well then, you're a fool. And you're a lousy doctor, too. Because I am crazy. *Quite* crazy."

"Of course you're crazy," Nursi said, also humoring him.

"And you, my dear, are rude to say such horrid things about your host. But sit down here, you two, and let me tell you something. Something of great value. Something that can make you *rich*."

We sat. He suddenly seemed quite a fascinating conversationalist.

"What was the first gift of Christmas?" Dr. Parken asked.

Oh, here we go again. "A parent's love for a child?" I ventured. I had read something about that somewhere recently.

"Christmas trees?" Nursi said. "Tinsel? A partridge in a pear tree?"

"No, no," Dr. Parken said. "Well, actually it wasn't a gift of Christmas. Doesn't have anything to do with Christmas at all. I just said that, because my mind tends to wander. But one of the first gifts given to the world was *infectious disease*. Pestilence! What would the Bible be without plagues and leprosy? What would the Middle Ages have been without the Black Death? Childhood has been robbed of its thrills by the loss of diphtheria, whooping cough, and smallpox. Doddering fogies like me hang around forever without what used to be called 'the old people's friend'—pneumonia—to carry us off."

"Gee, I never thought of that before," I said. In fact, I had a hard time thinking of it even now.

"Do you two want an endless career of hypertension, hemorrhoids, impotence, incontinence, and Alzheimer's?" Dr. Parken asked quietly.

He had a point. "Of course not," I said. "But what can we do? Thanks to the miracles of modern medicine, that's what a primary care physician's life has become."

"It doesn't have to be," Dr. Parken said. "I have the power to bring joy and prosperity back to your lives."

III. The Contagious Box

The next morning, Dr. Parken led us to a lovely old armoire, from which he extracted three sets of space suit–like protective garb.

"Put these on if you value your lives," he cautioned us.

We went upstairs, huffing and puffing through our respirator filters, passed through several hermetically sealed chambers with ultraviolet light and antiseptic showers, and then finally reached the attic.

"There it is," Parken said, pointing to a box in the corner. It was an intricately carved old walnut box, with a beautifully inlaid biohazard symbol on the lid.

"What's in it?" Nursi asked with some trepidation.

"Germs," Dr. Parken said. "Highly contagious, nasty, deadly germs."

He opened the lid. The box was a deceptive container, for the walnut outside was no more than decorative veneer covering a high-tech subzero freezer. Inside were nestled row after row of vials, each labeled with the name of some fearsome disease.

"The World Health Organization thought it did away with smallpox," Dr. Parken said triumphantly. "But I have a nice little batch here. It's one of the prizes of my collection." One after the other he lifted vials out of their plush nests, showing us their little labels, some lovingly decorated with miniature watercolor portraits of the bacteria they contained. "Leprosy," he said. "Bubonic plague. Typhoid. . . ." On and on he went.

"Where did you get all this?" I asked in wonder.

"I've been collecting them for years, my young friend. Whenever I had a patient with some particularly good infection, I kept a bit of phlegm or pus, a wee lump of flesh, or perhaps a tiny blood sample. I have dug around in the cemeteries, too, looking for bacteria that were buried with the people they had tried so hard to befriend."

"What will you do with these awful things?" Nursi asked.

"Why, I'm going to release them, of course!" our insane host replied. "On Christmas I will free some of my little friends into the world!"

"How dreadful! You are mad!" Nursi said.

I was frankly appalled. Nursi's lack of manners genuinely surprised me. She should hear our host out before making snap judgments.

"How will this bring us joy and prosperity?" I asked.

"Very simple," Parken replied. "These are not just any old infections. In my basement laboratory I have carefully manipulated them, bred them, cared for them, and turned them into antibiotic-resistant bacteria. These little darlings cannot easily be eradicated. But I have also developed vaccines. What I propose to do—what I propose for *us* to do—is to inoculate ourselves against these diseases, and then to release them, just a few at a time, very carefully."

"I'm afraid I don't really see the joy and prosperity in that, Dr. Parken. Perhaps I'm just slow," I said.

"You are slow. I've noticed that. But never mind. Just think: a world once more filled with barely treatable infectious disease. What, my young friend, will people need?"

IV. The Leprosarium

Maury Parken died in the spring. Not from an infectious disease, as he might have wished, but from what the coroner described as "literary necessity"—there was simply no more place for him in the story, whose plot turns required his demise.

Nursi and I overcame our narrow-minded objections to Dr. Parken's noble plan. As scientists, as objective medical professionals, we realized that the transcendent ideal in a democratic society is to achieve the greatest good for the greatest number. Bacteria, of course, exist in greater numbers than people. And then, too, we had to look out for ourselves, because those who do not love themselves are not capable of loving others. We figured we would work on the loving others part a little later, perhaps during our retirement, when we had the leisure to develop as full human beings in our Mediterranean villa, while the servants cleared the dishes and served us coffee and cognac on the veranda.

So we acquired all the old buildings at Saranac and refurbished them in preparation for the new outbreak of tuberculosis. We bought a leper colony down South that was on the verge of going out of business for lack of customers, and within two years we had turned it right around. We set up a chain of quarantine franchises—Germs "R" Us—throughout the United States, and picked up a nice piece of change on the side peddling surgical masks, latex gloves, and a full line of other protective paraphernalia.

Many years have passed, but we will never forget Dr. Parken and his fine gift, which we have come to call the Christmas Pox. So far we have only gone through six diseases. Many others are left.

The Christmas Box Lunch

he holidays mean lots of traveling. We here at the *New York Times* began to wonder how the many travelers of the First Christmas sustained themselves. So we asked a few of the country's best chefs to dream up the ideal Christmas Box Lunch for their favorite characters.

Christmas Box Lunch for the Three Wise Men, by Wolfgang Puck

Frankincense-grilled desert rat, chilled and served on a bed of Red Sea seaweed with a camel milk–coriander vinaigrette

Toasted chick peas

Papyrus-wheat pita bread pockets

Chocolate-covered figs with gold leaf served with almond-crusted star-shaped cookies

Christmas Box Lunch for King Herod, by Ann Rozensweig

Caesar salad with pistachio nuts

Personally slaughtered broiled baby lamb chops, marinated in wine and slave's blood

Deep-fried astronomer's eyeballs served with a Macedonian vinegar dipping sauce

Humble pie

Christmas Box Lunch for Mary and Joseph, by Georges Perrier

Placenta carpaccio with raw dove eggs

Oxtail soup with floating falafel balls

Happy Cuckold mini-loaves stuffed with olives, whitefish, and bitter herbs

Chocolate-covered matzohs

Christmas Box Lunch for the Shepherds, by Marcella Hazan

Sorrel salad with warmed sheep's milk cheese and toasted rosemary leaves

Angel food cake

The Christmas Boxer Shorts

 he advertisement in the newspaper leaped out at me:

SWF, 85, seeks young buck to rekindle her passion. There's life in the old girl yet! No contraceptives necessary.

I was having a hard time at home. My wife, Ovari, and I had been trying to have a baby for seven years. We tried everything—hormone shots, in vitro, and acupuncture. Ovari was desperate, emotionally clingy, and totally uninterested in any sex unless it could lead to motherhood. That's why the ad had caught my eye—here was an opportunity for me once again to play the young stud, without any procreational pressure. I had never cheated on Ovari before, but this sounded like fun. I couldn't resist.

I wrote to Melli at her P.O. Box and she called me the next week. I had to shout into the phone because she was hard of hearing, but even that didn't put me off—she sounded sexy, in an octogenarian sort of way. We arranged to meet at her place the next evening.

Let's get this straight—I normally don't like old ladies. They're boring and ill-dressed and sometimes even smell of urine. Melli was nothing like that. She was gorgeous. Even her wrinkles and folds of skin were elegant. She was the sexiest woman I've ever known. The moment I set eyes on her, all I could think of was, *When am I going to bed this lovely creature?*

It didn't take long. Melli and I went to the movies—a revival of *Harold and Maude* at the local university—and then for cappuccino afterwards. I had never met such a fascinating conversationalist. We talked long into the night about *film noir,* economic policy, and Nintendo. Before long we ended up at her planned living community, and I found myself under a down comforter in a room filled with memorabilia. The sex was hot—real hot—and there was no reproductive subtext. I loved it.

I had crawled home in the middle of the night—4 A.M., to be exact—and I told Ovari that I had car trouble. The next day I called in sick to work and spent the whole day ploughing Melli's infertile fields. The two of us were inseparable for weeks, with me spending hours in Melli's nostalgic bedroom learning all about the ancient Asian sex techniques she had picked up in the twenties when she was a missionary in China.

Then a sad day arrived. It was right before Christmas, as I recall. After one of the most mind-blowing orgasms I'd ever survived, Melli took me in her arms and told me she had important news. My thoughts went wild. Had she found another? Was she dumping me? Who was it? I would kill him!

"Henry, my dear... I'm dying," said my beloved. "In fact, they've told me I only have a few more weeks to live. You were my gift to myself. I wanted to feel a real man in my arms once again."

"No," I cried out, instantly dissolving into sobs. "No! You can't leave me. You're my perfect lover!"

Melli beamed beneficently. "You, my dear, are the sweetest thing! But I worry about you. I want you and your young wife to be happy. I'm leaving you a gift that will change your lives."

Melli and I made love fifteen more times that night, and in the morning she was dead, lying peacefully with a big smile on her delicate face.

I went home to a hostile Ovari, but I didn't care. I had lost the only woman who had reached me deeply both in my heart and in my gonads, and I was devastated.

Two days later, on Christmas Eve, a package arrived for me containing three dozen pairs of boxer shorts in every sort of pattern imaginable. Inside the box was Melli's last letter to me:

My dearest, dearest Henry,

You have given me the greatest joy I could have known in my final days—the joy of total womanhood.

And now I want to offer you an even better gift—the gift of fatherhood. I noticed, dear Henry, that you wear those tight, sexy Jockey shorts. I think that they might be impeding your spermatozoa. I have read studies that say boxer shorts lead to an increase in fertility. Please indulge an old lady in her last wish and try wearing the enclosed for a few weeks. Maybe you'll hear the pitter-patter of little feet around the house after all!

If the dead have sex dreams, please know that mine will all be about you!

Love and kisses,

Melli

What a woman! I spent the entire Christmas day trying on all the boxer shorts and recalling all of our wonderful times together. Then I had to wash all the boxer shorts, but it was worth it. After that I wore nothing but the big baggy underwear Melli had left me. Eventually Ovari and I reconciled, and within a couple of months she was pregnant.

And now, today, as I take my little girl Melli to the park with me, I can truly say that I know the meaning of Christmas.

THE CHRISTMAS PYRAMID

y wife, Phari, and I went on a little round-the-world jaunt a few years ago, leaving our seventeen young children with the neighbors.

In Egypt we took a tour of the pyramids. We were profoundly moved to see the mummy of an ancient ruler named Mary-hotep. Hieroglyphics on her mummy case admonished: "You should always take your children with you." And, in fact, Mary-hotep had done just that. Her entire family, all of her servants, and three hundred laborers had been killed and entombed with her.

We hurried home to New Jersey and began building our own pyramid, so that our family could be together forever.

The Wrong Christmas Box

by Robert Louis Stevens

ore than three centuries ago a Neapolitan banker, Lorenzo Tonti, conceived of the insidious financial scheme that will forever bear his name. Today we care little about Tonti, whose personal life time effectively erased. But his invention, the tontine, has wrought unspeakable havoc in fact and fancy ever since.

I could discuss the tontine system forever, but will not. A brief description should suffice. In its simplest form, a certain number of subscribers contribute identical sums of money to a fund intended to benefit either themselves or their heirs. The last surviving beneficiary receives the entire sum, plus whatever interest may have accrued in the meantime, and with luck has enough life left in him to enjoy it.

In one of its more recent incarnations, devised by a literary agent named Bob living in the shadow of the Wasatch Range near Salt Lake City, the stake was not mere cash, but the "Christmas Box." A hundred elderly, kindly, tragic figures—star-crossed lovers, widows and widowers, parents of long-dead children, separated Siamese twins, the Lost Dauphin, the Princess Anastasia, and so on—were the subscribers.

The supposed beneficiary would be posterity, as targeted through the medium of a young couple with a child seeking cheap lodgings while getting started in life. The winning subscriber would welcome this innocent family into an old mansion, play the sweet but dotty benefactor, and allow this family accidentally to "discover" the Christmas Box in the attic. The Christmas Box would, of course, be stocked with the winner's personal blend of bittersweet memories and moralistic platitudes, which would then be foisted on an unwitting and credulous society. In exchange for carrying out the oldster's plan, the young couple would receive a rose-gold timepiece and all print, electronic, film, and TV adaptation rights to the chosen story and any prequels, sequels, spin-offs, and so on. Bob, the agent who had devised the scheme in the first place, would, of course, get his 15 percent.

The years went by and, one after another, the original subscribers to the tontine perished. The precious contents that some wished to bequeath to posterity were forever lost. Al Capone withdrew all his valuables from his hidden safe, but never got to put them in his Christmas Box. Richard Nixon died without leaving behind his personal copy of the missing minutes from the Watergate tapes. Jimmy Hoffa was carrying his Christmas Box documents on that fateful evening.

Others grew tired of waiting and resorted to different outlets for their lust for immortality. An old lady in Madison County, Iowa, left the tale of some pathetic fling with a photographer to her children, who found another writer. A couple of other old ladies cobbled together their own memoirs. A few with acting pretensions got themselves humiliating gigs in incontinence or dietary fiber commercials on the sorry assumption that fleeting glory of any kind is preferable to dignified oblivion. Ronald Reagan became president, Frank Sinatra sang until he keeled over, and Bob Hope entertained troops until the military leaders of the world banded together and declared eternal peace in self-defense.

Eventually only two subscribers were left in the tontine, MaryLou Parking and her younger sister Nanette Parking, known affectionately as "Nono."

MaryLou's story involved a daughter who perished long ago, a clock collection, some Bibles, a marble angel, deep love, a brave stand against racial injustice, joy, sorrow, the whole nine yards, virtually guaranteed to flood Middle America with tears. It was fairly stuffed with moral fiber. It was heart-wrenching and perhaps even socially redeeming or inspiring for those who liked that sort of thing.

Nono's tale was rather different—a multigenerational saga of sex, crime, and dissipation on the Oregon Trail. The characters were hot, scantily clad babes and rugged, scantily clad guys. A few casting suggestions were included, should anyone contemplate a movie, though unfortunately Ronald Coleman and Clark Gable were no longer viable possibilities.

Tragically, MaryLou and Nono were killed simultaneously when they both tried to set records as the oldest solo transcontinental pilots and their airplanes collided in midair. Some call it kismet. One would like to imagine that they met again, for the first time in decades, on the way down, and perhaps effected some sort of reconciliation above the shrill blast of the wind.

Bob, the literary agent, was devastated. For generations he had groomed would-be writers to pose as the young couple who would tell the tontine winner's tale, and now the whole scheme seemed doomed. At first he thought of pretending that one or both of the sisters was still alive. The bodies, in fact, had never been recovered. But he quickly realized how wrong this would be. Why think so small? As long as he was pretending that dead people were alive, he might as well bring back *all* of the tontine members, claim that each was the last survivor, and begin a cottage industry of Christmas Box stories.

"Cottage" industry, in fact, is a misnomer: It was a condo industry. Bob assembled a group of backers and built Bob's Christmas Box Condos in Salt Lake City. Each unit in Bob's complex was sold to a writer represented by Bob, and each writer's unit had its own attic with its own Christmas Box. In one fell swoop, Bob had created an entire residential-entertainment empire.

Over the next few years, nine out of every ten books on the best-seller list were the product of Bob's Christmas Box writing mill. The scheme was so successful that Bob decided to start another tontine. And meanwhile, he devoted a portion of his vast income to a memorial to the tragic sisters whose demise helped make his fortune. This memorial garden, the Parking Lot, is located near the site of their crash and is open to the general public. Special memorial services are held every hour on the hour from 8 A.M. to 6 P.M., every day but Christmas. The rides and concessions run only from May 15 to October 15, but the souvenir shop and museum remain open all year.

Frosty Gump's
Big Christmas Box
of Christmas Cheer

i there! I'm Frosty Gump, the Christmas Imbecile.

I just love Christmas, don't you? My mama used to tell me it was the stupidest holiday ever, and I guess that's why I've always cottoned to it like no other day of the year. You know what my mom thinks stupid is? "Frosty," she always says. "Stupid is ordering a Christmas tree from L. L. Bean." Mama and I never have a tree—we just have Christmas sayings that we read, over and over again. You'll see them. You will. I keep them in my Christmas Box here. I got Mama to write 'em all down in a big list for you. I show 'em to people on park benches.

You know, over the years, I've gotten to know many Christmas celebrities. It seems like every time I turn around I have a brush with yuletide greatness, only I never really know it until someone shows me the videotape later on. Like, I think I was working as a shepherd when that Christ kid was born—who woulda thunk he'd turn out so famous? And I was living in Bedford Falls when Donna Reed and Jimmy Stewart made *It's a Wonderful Life*. You can see me in the background in the high school dance scene, showin' people my Christmas sayin's. I met a cowboy on a bus out of Austin one time, sang me a song about a reindeer with a shiny red nose. "Gene," I said, "kids will really love that song. I should know. I'm an imbecile." Then darn if I don't hear it on the radio a few months later.

Another time I ran into a guy who told me he had an idea for a big plastic bag to put under your tree—kinda like a garbage bag, only tree size. The man was a genius. I told him to try it, and look what happened.

One time a crazy thing happened: I found myself studying to be a monk in one of them there monasteries that makes Christmas fruitcakes. That's serious work. They was called Trappists, and I had gone there after seeing *The Sound of Music* 'cause I thought I was joining a singing family. But baking fruitcakes was exciting enough, I guess. I was the walnut brother, in charge of cracking all the walnuts. That was good. I'm glad I wasn't the candied cherry brother. They had to replace him every season 'cause he got fructose poisoning. And I'm glad I wasn't the stacking brothers—them fruitcakes was so heavy, the stacking brothers had to work out in a gym to lift boxes of 'em.

Yeah, I been lucky. Over the years I met nearly everyone who had anything to do with Christmas. Mel Tormé, nice white jazz singer, wanted to write something called "Hamhocks Roasting on an Open Fire." But I had just been one of the balloon handlers for the Macy's Thanksgiving Day parade in New York, where I saw lots of roasted chestnuts. I told Mel that "chestnuts" was more romantic. Yep.

The Christmas Sayings of Frosty Gump

- Life is like a box of Christmas candy—you never know who's gonna suck on your candy cane.

- A friendship is like a Christmas ornament—you gotta treat it right or it breaks.

- Life is like a stocking—you got to hang out to get the goodies.

- If you stand under the mistletoe too long, the berries drop off.

- It's better if people think you're a fruitcake than a turkey.

- Your brain is like a strand of Christmas lights—knock one part out, and everything starts to get blinky.

- Eggnog can never be too rich or too heavy.

- If you're fat and hairy, dress in red. It works for Santa.

- You can dream of a white Christmas, but black folks should get a holiday, too.

The Christmas Skinner Box

y wife, Goofi, and I used to have a terrible life. Being sloppy, maudlin human beings, we were buffeted by our emotions, which is terribly inefficient. What's worse, we seemed to be passing this on to our child, Jooni, who always clamored for attention and affection at the most inconvenient times. I was trying to run a store that sold overpriced educational playthings for children, for God's sake, and didn't have time for some damn brat always tugging at my sleeve yammering, "Play with me, daddy!" "Read to me, daddy!" "Help me decorate the Christmas tree, daddy!" How was I supposed to raise a child with this kind of nonsense going on?

Then Goofi saw an ad in the newspaper for a school that claimed to be based on sound behavioral scientific principles, and which guaranteed to turn your child into anything you wanted. We promptly went for an interview.

Mary, the proprietress, struck me as a dotty old lady, but she claimed to have studied with all the luminaries in the field.

"Pavlov could make dogs salivate at the sound of a bell!" she said.

"Well, that must have been very nice for Mr. Pavlov," I said, "assuming, of course, that he liked having dog spit all over his house. But that's not really what we were looking for."

"Foolish man! It's just an example," she chided.

I didn't much like being called foolish, even if I was. "Well, it's a pretty stupid example, if you ask me," I said.

"Skinner could make rats and pigeons do almost anything he wanted," she said.

"Let's get out of here, Goofi," I said, rising from my chair. "We wanted to domesticate Jooni, and now we're getting a menagerie!"

"No, no, you don't understand," Mary wailed. "If you can train animals, you can train people."

I sat. This was interesting. "Tell me more."

Mary explained rewards and punishment, positive and negative reinforcement, operant conditioning, chained responses, all the ways in which experience molds our way of dealing with the world.

"Learning from experience was the first gift to humans, enabling them to rise above dumb beasts," she said. "Now that we understand the mechanism, we can use nature's gift for our own purposes, to turn humans back into the dumb beasts we want."

She showed us the Skinner Box she kept in her attic.

"I raised my own child in this box," she said.

"What was her name?" Goofi asked.

Mary thought long. "I don't remember. In fact, I'm not sure that I ever gave her a name. Subjects' names have to be kept confidential, you know. But I have all the cumulative records of her responses. I'd be happy to show them to you."

"What happened to this child of yours?" I asked. I didn't care so much about the namby-pamby particulars of the process as I did about the final result.

Mary beamed radiantly. "She…" Mary paused. "He?" She paused

again. "Well, I don't remember, but whatever it was, it did very well. What, after all, do we want from our children? We want them to grow up independent of their parents. And my kid, whoever it was, grew up and moved out and I've never heard from it again. What more could a modern parent ask?"

Not much, I thought.

We enrolled Jooni. We never heard from her again. But we had the smug satisfaction of believing that the human race was better and more logical as a result of our acts.

The Christmas Bocks

his story isn't told nearly as often as it perhaps ought to be, but I guess that's understandable what with all the scandals in the military recently, not to mention the fact that it isn't very interesting in the first place. Still, it is a story, my story, or at least the best I can do at coming up with one.

Back in the early seventies I was stationed over in Germany, keeping the world safe from Communism. That mostly meant hanging out with my buddies and drinking a lot and driving real fast on the Autobahn and trying to get laid, and since Democracy is doing whatever the hell you want to do no matter what anybody else thinks, we were setting a good example for the rest of the world. Once in a while people called us Ugly Americans, but I think they were probably just talking about my friend Joe, who really is pretty ugly, I've got to agree, so I think they were just expressing an honest opinion and I have to respect them for it, even though we used to beat the crap out of them when they said it, because after all he was a friend and they were the enemy, or at least they had been in all the movies I had seen.

It was Christmas Eve and we were stuck in this washed-up, has-been Nazi country, just being the good guys, but at least a couple of us got leave from our nuclear missile launching facility, so we figured we would drive into town and get really shit-faced and maybe laid. Ho, ho, ho. So in about the fifth bar the bartender asks us if we'd ever had bock beer. We didn't know what the hell he was talking about and figured he was probably insulting us, so we were about to pound his face in when he said, "No, no, bock beer is a very good, strong, dark German beer." Well, that sounded okay and worth a try, so we drank about four gallons of the stuff apiece, and though it wasn't as good as the good old American brewskies we were accustomed to back home, it was better than nothing.

I don't know what bock beer is, but it does the job. We busted up one church service—they were singing some American Christmas carol but messing it all up and doing the words in German, the stinking krauts, so we went in singing "Yankee Doodle Dandy" and "Home on the Range" and stuff like that at the top of our lungs. They didn't seem to appreciate it very much, but of course they're foreigners and don't have any taste, so what can you expect? And then we went back to the base and decided we would give the damn Russkies an early Christmas present from Uncle Sam Claus right down the chimney of the Kremlin. We spent about an hour trying to guess the other half of the launch code for the missile before the military police came in and busted us.

In the end, then, nothing happened at all, except that we woke up with terrible hangovers the next day and spent a little time in the slammer. But imagine the possibilities. If we had figured out that code, which I admit was not very likely, then that one damn kraut bartender would have been responsible for making us start World War III. The Germans just won't stop, will they? But fortunately we couldn't figure it out, so we pulled the world back from the brink of nuclear disaster. Just another case of good old honest Americans doing their bit to make the world a better place.

So that was the story of the Christmas Bocks, and, even though it probably isn't much, that's all I've got.

THE CHRISTMAS BOXER

ary was a scrappy old bird, as we learned soon after moving into her mansion. Her broken nose and cauliflower ear indicated that she had a past. She was no angel, that's for sure.

"What do you suppose was the fourth gift of Christmas?" she asked me one evening over a third round of whiskies with beer chasers.

"Gold? Frankincense? Myrrh?" I replied.

"Those are three, you dumb lummox. What was the fourth?"

"Peace? Love? Giving?"

"Yeah, right. Dream on, Pollyanna."

"The love of a parent for a child?"

"Where do you get this crap? Did you read it somewhere, or does it come out of your very own head?"

"Ummmmm."

"Look, little Mr. Goody Two-shoes, the first three kings brought gold and those other things you talked about. And then the fourth king, Don King, brought the fights."

"The fights?"

"You bet. The fights. Started out in the Colosseum, but it didn't catch on too well. The matches were too short. You know, that float like a butterfly sting like a bee stuff doesn't work too well against a lion or a gladiator."

"I guess not."

"No, but he persisted. And after two thousand years he made it to Madison Square Garden and pay-per-view. A real success story."

"I never knew that."

"Yeah, well, now you do."

"That's a very touching story, Mary. Do you mind if I write a book about it? I think it would be a bestseller."

"Be my guest, pal."

THE CHRISTMAS LOX,

OR A RIVER OF CREAM CHEESE RUNS THROUGH IT

hen I was a very little boy, my father, Daddi, taught me fly-fishing. He also taught my older brother, who was nicknamed "Fishi" and grew up to look exactly like Brad Pitt. Together, the three of us would spend at least twelve hours a day wading around mountain streams in our silly-looking giant galoshes that look like whole-body condoms. Then, as the sun was setting in the vast Montana sky, we would head home with our catch of salmon and trout, where we would invariably be met by piercing screams from our mother, Mommi.

"Get that stinking fish out of the house!" she would shriek. Mommi hated to cook, and she hated fish. Back then there weren't any microwave ovens and we only had a tiny freezer. So our backyard was filled with stinking piles of rotting fish flesh. Since we usually caught over a dozen a day, some of the piles were over eight feet tall. You would think that this would stop us from fishing, but think again. We were addicted to the hobby. Mommi tried everything to discourage us, including poking holes in our galoshes, but we were manly men and we had to fish and silently brood all day long or we wouldn't have been fulfilling our genetic destiny.

Our house had lovely gardens around it from all the rotting fish fertilizer, but no one came to see us because of the smell. But there was a plus side—twenty mountain lions camped out in our yard, munching on the piscine goodies. They were totally tame—my whole childhood was just like that movie *Born Free,* except that it smelled more like the Dead Sea than the Serengeti Plain.

From time to time, Daddi would get miffed at Mommi and try to get her to do her wifely duty when it came to the fish. "You could pickle it," he would say. "How about smoking it?" Mommi held steadfast—she did not come from fish-cooking people. "Fish is brain food," she would say, "and you know that low IQs have always run in my family."

Our lives changed one day when an itinerant peddler followed his nose and made a house call.

"Fish!" exclaimed the little Jewish man, who was lugging along a cart filled with pots, pans, and a big heaping basket of bagels. "It's my favorite food!"

We learned that his name was Gefilti, and that he had been inland for twenty years without tasting fish flesh.

"Well, you've come to the right place," said Daddi. "Help yourself—the fresh stuff's on the top of the pile."

"How much?" asked Gefilti the Peddler.

"Oh, it's free, my good man," said Daddi. "My wife won't cook it anyway. Says she doesn't like fish."

"Doesn't like fish? Doesn't she know it's brain food?"

"I'm afraid she knows. Maybe she thinks that if she got smarter, she wouldn't want to live out here in the middle of nowhere in Montana where grown men wade around in streams all day. At least that's my charitable interpretation. Maybe she's just too stupid to cook," said Daddi ruefully.

"She just needs motivation," said Gefilti, springing into action. From out of his cart he produced an ornately carved wooden box with a Star of David on top.

"What's that?" asked my brother Fishi.

"This is a Hanukkah Box," said Gefilti. "I keep everything that is most precious to my family in this box. This is the box with the lox."

"It's not locked," I said. "Look. It opens right up."

"No, no! *Lox.* You poor child, don't you know from smoked salmon? This box contains the recipe for the best lox you'll ever eat outside a *shtetl.* I've been traveling around for years in search of some fish to use it on."

"You see, I told my wife she should smoke the fish, or pickle it," said Daddi.

"Leave it to me. When I get going, she'll be *begging* for that lox recipe," said Gefilti. Then he set to work cleaning and cutting scores of salmon. He built a lean-to and inside set a wonderful crisp-burning fire of hickory wood. He followed his recipe to the last word and produced what he called "first-rate lox—better than Nova!"

The next morning he brought Mommi a breakfast tray in bed. He had fixed a heaping plateful of bagels with mounds of cream cheese. On top of one of the bagels was a teeny-weeny piece of lox no bigger than a fingernail.

"What's that pink thing?" asked Mommi suspiciously.

Gefilti clucked his tongue. "Oh, nothing you'd want to eat. It's too good to waste on you anyway. It's like gold! Let me take it away."

"Wait!" she said, grabbing the piece of smoked salmon suddenly and popping it in her mouth. Her eyes bulged with pleasure. "Umm. What is this?"

"I'm sorry. There's no more of it," snapped Gefilti, bounding back downstairs. He repeated this performance the next morning, and then the next, each day giving Mommi just a tad more lox. Soon she was addicted to it and begging for the stuff.

"I'll give you all the lox you want," the Jewish peddler told her, "if only you'll be a good wife and learn how to make it for your husband."

Mommi agreed, and she and Gefilti set out to smoke every single fish we took out of the river after that. They formed the Christmas Lox Company, which shipped smoked salmon, trout, and paddlefish all around the world—they gave Harry and David and the Wisconsin Cheeseman a run for their money when it came to mail-order food goodies.

We were all happy. Finally, the fish were being used, and we were getting rich. Then things started going bad. Fishi was killed by the local townspeople when he got drunk one night and tried to check into a motel with his giant trout girlfriend. They didn't think a trout was good enough for a boy who looked like Brad Pitt.

And Gefilti, too, met a terrible fate. The mountain lions who had been living for years on the rotting piles of fish began to get restless and menacing, even though Mommi still threw them a few scraps now and then. One night, as Gefilti was going to the outhouse, the male of the pride nabbed him and started to bite his head off. His screaming woke me up, and I heard his last words: "But you're supposed to eat Christians, you *meshuggener* cat!"

Mommi and Daddi kept the Christmas Lox Company going for a little while after that, but they got sick of all the paperwork and opened up a petting farm featuring mountain lions. They commissioned Claes Oldenburg to do a giant marble statue of a bagel, cream cheese, and lox in memory of our dear friend Gefilti who taught us the lesson of the Christmas Lox.

THE CHRISTMAS SAFE-DEPOSIT BOX

Announcer

Tonight on *Rinaldo!*—the exciting story of the Christmas Safe-Deposit Box. And here is your host, the one, the only, Rinaldo Guevera!

Rinaldo

Here we are in the former Hometown First National Bank building. The Hometown Bank went out of business forty years ago—it was about the only bank in the world to go bust during the boom years of the fifties—and the building has been vacant ever since. Now this young couple, Richie and Moni Richards—say hello, Richie and Moni....

Richie

Hello.

Moni

Hello.

Rinaldo

...Richie and Moni have bought this bank building and are renovating it as their home. The renovation process itself will

be the subject of a multipart PBS series cohosted by Louis
Rukeyser and Bob Vila called *This Old Money Pit.* But tonight
we are here for a different reason. While surveying their new
property, Richie and Moni discovered, way down in the back
of the vault, an old safe-deposit box that had been left behind.
The box was locked. What was your first thought, Richie?

Richie

We thought maybe it was full of money or jewels.

Moni

But we picked it up and shook it and it felt empty.

Richie

Ssssssshhhhh! Ahem! As I was saying, Rinaldo, we thought it
might be full of something valuable, but then we figured its
value might be measured in something more than just mate-
rial worth.

Rinaldo

You thought of the entertainment value, of course.

Richie

Of course.

Rinaldo

And so...

Moni

And so we offered to sell it to you for $60,000, which we
thought would help pay for the renovation of the building.

Rinaldo

Right. Well, enough of that. We also have with us master safe-cracker Robbi Sutton, released from prison after novelist Norman Mailbox interceded with the authorities and wrote a bestselling book about his sadly misunderstood career. How are you, Robbi?

Robbi

Just great, Rinaldo. I'm really looking forward to this.

Rinaldo

Good, Robbi, good. So is everyone in America. But first, let's cut away to a commercial.

Rinaldo

Well, here we are back again. Robbi has his Christmas Toolbox with him and has started working away at the lock. If all else fails—which we hope it doesn't—he also has a Christmas Box of Dynamite and will blast the sucker open.

Robbi

Uh, well, it's open, Rinaldo. Actually it wasn't locked in the first place, just a little rusty.

Rinaldo

This is very exciting. So what's in there, Robbi?

Robbi

Nothing, Rinaldo.

Rinaldo

Now let's not be pessimistic, Robbi. You know that old thing about the glass being half full or being half empty, don't you? Well, let's not put ourselves in the half-empty-glass crowd, Robbi, because I don't think the viewing audience would like that too much.

Robbi

Well, Rinaldo, usually I would put myself in the half-full-glass crowd. But this time I just can't. Let me put it this way: If you had somebody who didn't understand what emptiness was, and you wanted to explain it to them, well, this safe-deposit box would be a very good visual aid.

Rinaldo

There's *nothing* in it?

Robbi

El zilcho.

Rinaldo

Dust, maybe? Or a dead insect? You know, in *Jurassic Park* they recreated whole dinosaurs from DNA in dead insect blood, so even a dead bug could be stuffed with earth-shattering significance.

Robbi

No dust. No bugs. Nada.

Rinaldo

Nothing. Nothing. Ah, you say there's nothing. But isn't

nothingness itself something? Nothingness is a void. Like the void that existed at the beginning of creation, when God said, 'Let there be light.'

Robbi

Well, I don't know, Rinaldo, I don't see any of that in here.

Rinaldo

You can leave now, Robbi.

[Pause.]

The *Void* is potential. The Void holds all that *might* be. The void in this box, which seems like nothing, holds the possibility of being *everything*.

Robbi

Uh, Rinaldo, the box is *empty*.

Rinaldo

I said you can *leave* now, Robbi. Your work is done. Pick up your check at the door.

[Pause.]

Nothing, of course, is ever truly empty. Aside from the Void, pregnant with the potential birth of the Universe, this box contains air. Air. *Air.* What is air? Air is one of the four elements. Air is a basic requisite of life. Air is everywhere. And what is this particular air that we find within this box, left to us, to posterity, by some unknown benefactor? Why did this person leave us this air? What is its significance? What hidden meaning does it hold—for it must be of incredible value for someone to have locked it away in a safe-deposit box for forty years! Is this the air that George Washington breathed during that cold winter at Valley Forge? Is this the air inspired by those who drafted the Declaration of Independence? Or is it the last breath of Thomas Edison, of Newton, of Beethoven, of Shakespeare? Is it the gentle breeze that separated wheat from chaff for generations of laboring peasants, or the warm Aegean wind that filled the sails of the ship that carried Helen off to Troy? This may be the air of the pharaohs, the air of Cro-Magnons, the air that greeted the first fish that crept from the sea or that wafted through the Garden of Eden. I do believe, viewers, that we have been privileged to discover, right here, tonight, in this humble safe-deposit box, both the void of potential and the primordial air that are all things, at all times, to everyone, everywhere. Remember, you saw it first on *Rinaldo!*

And that's our show. Thanks for tuning in.

Sequels, Fabulous Sequels

Don't miss these great sequels

- **THE CHRISTMAS FUSEBOX** A family discovers that a secret box in the basement holds the key to the mystery of the flickering Christmas lights.

- **THE CHRISTMAS BOX TURTLE** The touching tale of a young family's love for its reptile and the terrible fate it meets beneath the wheels of an EPA inspector's truck.

- **THE CHRISTMAS CIGARETTE BOX** A young couple moves into the home of R. J. Reynolds.

- **THE CHRISTMAS JURY BOX** A Christmas reunion special featuring the O. J. jurors, Marcia Clark, Johnnie Cochran, Christopher Darden, Judge Lance Ito, and O. J. himself singing "I'm Dreaming of a White Bronco."

- **THE CHRISTMAS BOXCAR CHILDREN** Classic stories retold for the holiday season.

- **THE CHRISTMAS BOOM BOX** The big book of holiday rap lyrics.

- **THE CHRISTMAS WOK** Peking turkey, stir-fried stovetop stuffing, and other Asian-influenced holiday recipes.

- **THE CHRISTMAS BOX KITE** A fanciful recreation of Benjamin Franklin's electrical experiments.

- **THE CHRISTMAS BOX SPRING** The strange yet poignant marriage of an insomniac nymphomaniac and a narcoleptic.

- **THE CHRISTMAS SQUEEZEBOX** Lively carols set to a polka beat.

- **THE CHRISTMAS STRONGBOX** The holidays come early, and with a big bang, to the Hole-in-the-Wall gang.

- **THE IKEA CHRISTMAS BOX CATALOG** Self-assembled boxes of memories. Choose from many models, including Jenna, Keri, Lauri, and Danica.

- **THE BOX LESS OPENED** by M. Scott Pack. Life lessons for those who long to unpack life's mysteries.

- **MARS AND VENUS IN A CHRISTMAS BOX** Gender-related gift-buying and gift-giving tips.

- **SEVEN CHRISTMAS BOXES OF HIGHLY EFFECTIVE PEOPLE** How leaders wrap their presents.

And don't forget—Christmas Box–inspired television fare on

THE CHRISTMAS BOX NETWORK

▓ **MARRIED...WITH BOXES** The hilarious sitcom about a working couple constantly getting transferred.

▓ **BAYBOX** The gripping drama set in the gift-wrapping section of a San Francisco department store.

▓ **THE X-BOXES** Who are they, and where do they come from? Intriguing stories about extraterrestrial boxes.

▓ **AMERICA'S MOST WANTED BOXES** Is it the shoebox, the hatbox, or the mailbox? Call up and let us know!

▓ **MELROSE BOX** A trendy evening soap about the homeless.

▓ **BEVERLY BOX 38-24-38** A young, lithe teenager lives in a locker at Beverly Hills High.

▓ **AMERICA'S FUNNIEST HOME BOXES** Viewer's choices of the funniest and most poignant boxed moments of their lives—the baby crawling into a box, the dog puking in a box, spouses being carried out in a box.

▓ **BOX BLOOPERS** It's amazing, the howling hilarity, when things go wrong with boxes.

▓ **THIS OLD CHRISTMAS BOX** Two handymen set out to restore old packing crates to pristine condition.

▓ **BOXES OF THE RICH AND FAMOUS** See Imelda Marcos's shoeboxes, Paul Newman's popcorn boxes, Courtney Love's pillboxes, and Marlon Brando's iceboxes.